F
1435
.T8713
1993

Tutor, Pilar.

Mayan civilization.

$20.00

4/96

THE WORLD HERITAGE

MAYAN CIVILIZATION

UNESCO

CP CHILDRENS PRESS ®

CHICAGO

Table of Contents

Library of Congress Cataloging-in-Publication Data
Tutor, Pilar
  [Pueblo Maya. English]
  Mayan Civilization / by Pilar Tutor.
    p. cm. — (The World heritage)
    Includes index.
    Summary: An introduction to the culture of the ancient Mayas, discussing
political and social organization, daily life, traditions, religion, and cities.
    ISBN 0-516-08381-3
    1. Mayas—Juvenile literature. [1. Mayas. 2. Indians of Central America.] I. Title.
II. Series.
F1435.T87 1993
972.81'016—dc20
                              92-37022
                              CIP

El Pueblo Maya: © INCAFO S.A./Ediciones S.M./UNESCO 1988
Mayan Civilization: © Childrens Press, Inc./UNESCO 1993

ISBN (UNESCO) 92-3-102589-9
ISBN (Childrens Press) 0-516-08381-3

3

Mayan Civilization

We have known of Mayan culture since 1517, when the Spaniard Francisco Hernández de Córdoba invited two Maya Indians to dine aboard his ship. This was the first attempt to unravel the mysteries of this culture, many of which remain unsolved to this day. Later, Hernández de Córdoba was killed in battle by the Maya.

Little is known about the Maya during their earliest days. For at least 3,000 years, some lived as nomadic hunters and gatherers, while others settled in small villages. This is known as the Mayas' Formative Period. The Classic Period of Mayan civilization began about A.D. 300. Around A.D. 600 began the highly civilized Late Classic Period. After the Spanish conquistadores *arrived in the sixteenth century, bringing with them war and disease, Mayan civilization came to an end.*

The Maya settled along the rivers and lakes of the Petén region of present-day Guatemala and Honduras. In Guatemala, they built such cities as Tikal and Quiriguá. Copán arose in the land that is now Honduras.

Little by little, the Maya expanded to the north until they established power in the Yucatán peninsula. There they founded the city of Chichen Itzá and formed alliances with the cities of Uxmal and Mayapán. The so-called Mayapán League endured until the fifteenth century, when all of Mayan civilization was sliding into a decline.

When the Spaniards arrived, the Maya lived in many small cities that fought constantly among themselves. This internal strife made the Spanish conquest much easier. Nevertheless, the Maya continued to resist Spanish domination for more than two hundred years. In many areas of the Yucatán, Maya is still the primary language.

Annals of the City

Stelae are great blocks of stone, with the figure of a man usually carved on one side. The other sides bear inscriptions with the dates when various cities were founded and with the exploits of powerful rulers. The stela in the photo stands in the city of Quiriguá. Quiriguá was founded around the year 650 and abandoned in the tenth century.

Political and Social Organization

The Maya lived in many independent cities, each with its own government. The highest authority in the city was the *halach uinic*, a Maya word that means "true man." With the help of his advisers, the chiefs and priests, he handled the city's internal and external affairs.

The chiefs were known as the *bataboob*. Below them were many lesser officials who kept the city running smoothly.

Priests were persons of great importance in Maya life. They were considered members of the nobility. Only the priests knew the mysteries of astronomy, mathematics, and the calendar. With this knowledge, they were able to declare the proper times for planting and harvesting. This was important to a society that depended on agriculture for its survival. Priests guided all religious ceremonies and rituals, and they also served as doctors and oracles. The high priest was called the *ahuacán*, and the many priests below him were known as *chilanés*.

The Maya Metropolis
Tikal had some 10,000 inhabitants. The population may have been as high as 50,000 if the neighborhoods on the outskirts are counted. For a time, Tikal was the Mayas' chief ceremonial center. Today about 3,000 buildings and other structures are preserved in an area of 6 square miles (16 square kilometers). The temple in the photo at the right, measuring 230 feet (70 meters) high, was one of the tallest structures in Pre-Columbian America. It is one of many temples to be seen in Tikal today.

The Last Stelae
Quiriguá is famous for its spectacular stelae, which have been named by letters of the alphabet. The stela at the left is known to archaeologists as K. Stelae K and I were among the last to be erected in the city. Both date from early in the tenth century.

Remains of Quiriguá

Quiriguá was founded as a satellite city to Copán, 30 miles (48 kilometers) away. Like Copán and Tikal, Quiriguá reached its high point during the eighth century A.D. Unfortunately, its buildings are badly deteriorated today, and little of the ceremonial center has been preserved. The plaza, altars, temples, and stelae are in ruins. The photograph shows the remains of Temple V.

Religion was a vital force for the Maya. The gods gave them health and food. Ceremonies to calm the anger of the gods often involved sacrificial ritual. Human sacrifice was sometimes part of Maya religious practices.

The *memba uinicoob,* or common people, worked the land. With their labor, they fed and maintained the priests and nobles. They built temples and ball courts and paid tribute to the chiefs.

The lowest position in the Maya hierarchy was occupied by the *pentacoob,* or slaves. A person could become a slave by being taken prisoner in war or by being sold in the market.

The Maya lived by farming and trading. Their cornfields were known as *milpas.* To prepare the land for planting, they cut down the trees and underbrush and burned them. When the land was cleared, they planted their grain.

Since the land rapidly lost its fertility, the people of a Maya settlement had to move every few years. Today, many peasants of Guatemala, Mexico, and Honduras still use this system.

The Descendants of the Maya

In Mexico's Yucatán peninsula and in the Mexican state of Chiapas live the Lacandones. They are among the last indigenous groups that still cling to their ancient customs, despite the intrusion of the outside world.

There are two Lacandon groups. The northern group lives near the ruined Mayan city of Palenque. The southern Lacandones live around the ancient city of Yaxchilan. Both groups speak a Mayan dialect. Their language and their extremely rich oral tradition prove that the Lacandones are closely related to the ancient Maya, who flourished more than a thousand years ago.

The Lacandones still wear their traditional costume, a cotton tunic called the *xikul.* They go barefoot, wear their hair very long, and carry a leather pouch known as the *pooxah.*

The present-day Lacandones live much as their ancestors did before them. They rise early to tend their cornfields, or *milpas.* They cultivate the land by the ancient method of slashing and burning. They cut down the trees, burn away the underbrush, plant, harvest, and move on to new

land every few years. Their houses have wooden walls and roofs of spiny palm. The houses have no windows, but their many doors let in light and fresh air.

The Lacandon religion is similar to that of the Maya. It involves the same gods, rituals, and ceremonies. However, the Lacandones have simplified some of the complicated practices of their ancestors. They have also combined some ancient beliefs and rituals with those of Roman Catholicism.

Today the Lacandon population totals only about four hundred people. The whole community is in danger of disappearing forever. Their environment is being destroyed by the construction of new highways and by slash-and-burn agriculture. Dealers pay high prices for mahogany, *guayamán,* cedar, and other valuable timber that grows in the jungle. All these factors are reducing the once-fertile land to a desert.

Fortunately, however, there is an international effort to create a huge preserve to protect the environment and the native peoples of the Yucatán.

Supernatural Animals
Zoomorphs are stone sculptures that depict mythical animals. An altar stands beside each zoomorph. The top photo at the right shows the largest zoomorph that survives today.

The Maya had a unique numbering system, as shown in the drawing below.

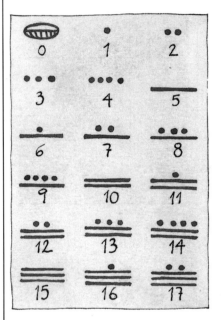

Struggle against the Jungle
The lower-right photo shows a glimpse of the complex tropical rain forest. The Maya were very resourceful in obtaining what they needed from the tropical environment.

In addition to corn, the Maya raised kidney beans, squash, and avocados. They completed their diet with fish and the meat of wild animals. They had no beasts of burden and few domestic animals of any kind. They did raise a breed of dog, feeding it so that they could eat it themselves later on. They also kept such domesticated birds as the turkey, duck, dove, and partridge.

To obtain goods they couldn't produce, the Maya traded with other Indian groups. Skilled craftspeople turned raw materials into objects that could be traded.

Daily Life

When a woman wanted to have a child, she consulted a priest and prayed to Ixchel, the goddess of pregnancy and childbirth. The birth of a baby was an occasion for celebration and feasting. In a special ceremony called the *paal*, the umbilical cord was cut and the child was given a name. In another part of this ceremony, small boards were fastened to the baby's head, meant to deform it for life.

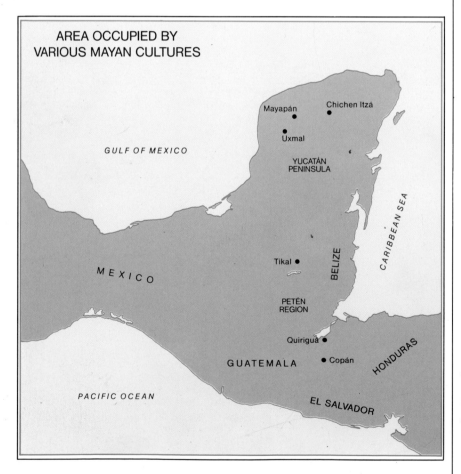

AREA OCCUPIED BY VARIOUS MAYAN CULTURES

GULF OF MEXICO

Mayapán

Chichen Itzá

Uxmal

YUCATÁN PENINSULA

MEXICO

CARIBBEAN SEA

Tikal

BELIZE

PETÉN REGION

Quiriguá

GUATEMALA

Copán

HONDURAS

PACIFIC OCEAN

EL SALVADOR

Images of the Elite

The stelae at Copán almost always depicted men in elaborate costume, full of symbolic images. These figures wear plumes on their heads, and belted aprons from which hang small pouches. The hands often hold a stick or a small box. The luxurious clothing shows that these images represent people of high rank or political power. In fact, they are named as the rulers or "kings" of these cities. Copán's Stela B, shown in the photo, is one of the best preserved stelae in existence today.

Throughout their history, the Maya settled along rivers and lakes in the Petén and Yucatán regions. Little by little they expanded to the north, until they reached the northern part of the Yucatán peninsula.

From the time they were very young, both boys and girls were directed toward their future roles in society. Thus, when they were three or four months old, they were shown all the equipment they would need in adult life.

Young boys were presented with the tools they would need as fathers. Little girls were shown the household utensils they would use in their future role as wife and mother.

When they became teenagers, boys and girls went through special coming-of-age ceremonies. After these rituals, they were considered adults, eligible for marriage.

Mothers taught their daughters to be modest, to bow their heads before men. Girls learned how to make corn tortillas, to wash clothes, and to care for the home. Fathers taught their sons to be honorable and obedient and to respect their elders and their ancestors.

When young people wanted to marry, their parents hired a matchmaker. The matchmaker looked for an appropriate woman or man, preferably from the same town and of the same social class.

Next, the two families agreed upon a dowry. This was a gift or payment from the bride's family to the groom. When everything was arranged, the wedding was celebrated with a great feast.

Before they married, boys used black paint on their faces and bodies. After marriage, they painted their bodies red, and only used black when they took part in religious ceremonies.

The Maya family rose very early. Women got up at three or four o'clock in the morning to prepare breakfast, which consisted of tortillas and beans. First the men ate, and later, when they had gone to the *milpas,* it was the women's turn.

While the men worked in the fields, the women cleaned house and made tortillas for the noon meal. Everyone ate when the men returned. The husbands then enjoyed a bath, which the women had prepared.

After the noon meal, the men were busy with community projects, such as the building of temples. Dinner time was about seven in the evening. Between eight and nine, everyone went to bed. The whole family slept in the same room.

Maya men wore a loincloth, or *ex,* and a light shawl, or *patí,* over their shoulders. They plaited their hair in a long braid. Women wore a loose, white dress called the *kub.* Like the men, they had very long hair, which they arranged in various styles.

Both men and women adorned themselves with earrings, nose rings, and body paint on special occasions.

Copán and Quiriguá

Copán was an important Mayan city. It was located on the Copán River in the Petén region in western Honduras. Quiriguá was an extension, or "vassal city," of Copán. Ironically, these two cities are now separated by an international border, for Quiriguá lies in Guatemala. The photographs show views of both cities. *(Top right)* The Acropolis of Copán, a collection of ancient pyramids, terraces, and temples. *(Bottom right)* The Plain of Stelae in Quiriguá. Quiriguá has thirteen monuments of this type.

14

The Maya also deliberately deformed their bodies as a sign of beauty and to indicate social status. One such mark of beauty was skull deformation. The process had to begin when a child was only four or five days old.

Small boards were fastened to the baby's forehead and to the back of its head with tight cords. As the baby grew, its skull followed the lines of the boards. Its head was thus flattened for life.

To be cross-eyed was also a sign of beauty. Mothers hung a little ball of resin from their child's hair in the front. The ball dangled between the baby's eyes, so that the child constantly turned its eyes inward.

When a person became ill, a priest was called in. The priest used a variety of remedies, from herbs to prayers. If the person died, the body was wrapped in a shroud. The mouth was filled with ground corn and quantities of jade. The body would use this as food on the long journey to the Kingdom of Death.

Poor people were buried beneath their houses. The houses were abandoned when the last inhabitants finally died. Nobles were cremated, and their ashes were sometimes stored in urns beneath the temples.

Cradle of the Sages
Copán was a major cultural and intellectual center. Here, as in other major centers, the Maya conducted scientific and mathematical investigations. In Copán, the Maya designed their famous calendars and perfected their hieroglyphic writing. All this knowledge was in the hands of the priests, while the common people worked the fields. The priests helped the farmers with their knowledge of astronomy and the seasons. The farmers, in turn, supported the priests with their labor. The Mayas' main crop was corn, but they also grew kidney beans, squash, potatoes, and avocados.

The Gods

Religion was extremely important to the Maya. When they asked the gods for favors, they made elaborate sacrifices. On occasion, they sacrificed human beings.

The Maya believed that the earth rested on the back of a crocodile that floated in a great lagoon. Over this lagoon hung the thirteen skies, the lowest of which was the earth. Beneath the earth were nine lower worlds. Each of the skies and the lower worlds was ruled by a god. The Maya were devoted to the gods, for they bestowed health and food.

The most important gods were: Itzamna, lord of life; Ali Kin, the sun god; Ah Puch, god of death; Chac, god of water and rain; Yumkax, the corn god; and Ixchel, goddess of the moon, of pregnancy, and of abundance.

Later the Mayan god Kukulkán, the feathered serpent, was created from Quetzalcoatl, a god of the Aztecs of Mexico. In addition, there were a host of lesser gods, such as the patrons of the days and months.

Sacrifices were made to the gods when something very important was at stake, such as the need to avoid a drought. The Maya offered the gods food, pottery, animals, or sometimes even humans. Animals such as deer, dogs, and turkeys were typical sacrifices.

The blood of the sacrificial victim was sprinkled on the statues of the gods. The Maya believed that the gods used blood as food.

Zoomorphs and Temples

The zoomorphs of Quiriguá date from a later period than the stelae. They must have had very special significance, for the Maya revered everything that pertained to the gods and the supernatural world. *(Top photo)* A zoomorph altar in Copán. *(Bottom photo)* The spectacular view from the terrace of the main temple at Tikal.

Timeline of Mayan History

A.D. 36	Stela 1 from El Baul is earliest dated Mayan monument.
c. 300	Beginning of the Classic Period of Mayan history
c. 400	Teotihuacan people of Mexico invade, introducing their own architecture and ideas.
c. 600	Teotihuacan influence permeates Maya lands; beginning of the Late Classic Period of Mayan history
638	Lord Pacal (Hand-shield), the greatest lord of Palenque, dies and is buried in the temple of the inscriptions.
c. 650	Quiriguá is founded.
700s	Tikal, Copán, and Quiriguá are at their peak.
c. 800	The magnificent polychrome Bonampak murals are painted.
900s	Tikal, Copán, Quiriguá, and other cities in the Petén region are abandoned. A group settles at Chichen Itzá.
1000s	Founding of the Mayapán League
1400s	Collapse of the Mayapán League
1517	Spaniards first arrive in the Yucatán area. The Spanish leader, Hernández de Córdoba, is killed by Mayan warriors.
1528	The Spanish conquest of the Maya begins under the direction of Francisco de Montejo.
1542	Merida, the Spanish capital of the Yucatán, is founded.
1697	Defeat of the last independent Maya city, Tayasal
1712	The Tzeltal Maya lead a major revolt against Spaniards.
1868	Another major revolt by the Tzeltal Maya

19

The Grand Plazas of Copán

Five esplanades, or wide walkways, have been discovered in Copán. They are actually great plazas that, with the Acropolis, form the heart of the ruined city. The Ceremonial Esplanade is a stadium about 800 square feet (75 square meters) in size. The Central Esplanade seems to be the most important, due to its central position. The Esplanade of the Hieroglyphic Stairway opens to a gigantic staircase that leads to the sanctuary. Last are the Eastern and Western Esplanades, courtyards of the Acropolis. The photo shows one of the altars of the Esplanade of the Hieroglyphic Stairway.

Human sacrifice took several forms. The heart could be cut from the victim, he could be hurled from a cliff, or he could be thrown down a deep well in order to speak with the water gods. Like the Aztecs of Mexico, the Maya believed the most valuable offerings to the gods were human blood and lives.

Writing, Numbers, and the Calendar

The Maya wrote with symbols called hieroglyphs. Magnificent stone pillars called stelae, carved with hieroglyphs and dates, record events such as births, deaths, wars, and marriages of important people. Hieroglyphic writing also appears on the walls of buildings and on ceramic vases. Mayan scholars are now figuring out the sentence structure of hieroglyphic writings and thus reading Mayan history.

It is hard to tell who among the Maya could read and write. Certainly, the scribes did both. Probably some, if not most, of the noble class were able to read. However, it is not likely that the common people could read.

The Maya were highly skilled in mathematics. They could divide fractions and work logarithms. They were among the earliest people to discover the concept of zero. Priests were proficient at mathematics, while the common people used simple arithmetic.

City beneath the Fields
The ruins of Quiriguá were discovered totally by accident in the middle of the nineteenth century. A family decided to clear some of its land for farming. When they started to plow, they found the first archaeological remains. Excavations did not actually begin until 1910, under the American Geological Institute. The city was divided evenly into neighborhoods, or barrios. The photograph shows two of the many altars found in the city.

Important Mayan Terms

ahuacán: high priest

bataboob: chief

chilán: priest

ex: loincloth

halach uinic: highest authority of the city

katún: period of twenty years

kub: woman's dress

memba uinicoob: common people

paal: ceremony after the birth of a child

patí: shawl worn over the shoulders

pentacoob: slaves

tlachtli: ball game

The Maya used two very accurate calendars. One, the *Haab,* had 360 days, plus five "days of ill fortune." The *Haab* ruled daily life. The other calendar, the *Tzolkín,* had 260 days and governed the religious ceremonies. The Maya calendars were probably more accurate than those used in Europe during the same time period.

Artistic Activities

As in other areas of Maya life, art was subject to religion and guided by the priests. The most spectacular architectural achievements include fields for playing ball, houses, astronomical observatories, bridges, aqueducts, and temples in the form of terraced pyramids. The outsides of important buildings were adorned with intricate stone-carved decoration.

Few examples of painting have been preserved. Nevertheless, the frescoes in the city of Bonampak are outstanding.

Maya potters worked clay with their hands. Vases have been found with multi-colored scenes painted on them. The Maya also fashioned artworks from stone, bone, flint, and jade.

Unanswered Questions
On the rear side of Mayan stelae are intriguing hieroglyphs. For many years, their meaning was totally unknown. Today, scholars know that the stelae inscriptions represent important events in the lives of the leaders of Mayan society. They may denote ascension to the throne, a famous battle, or a birth or death in the royal family. In the photo is the rear side of Stela F of Copán.

The costume of the common people was extremely simple. Yet people took great pains with their attire when they attended festivals. In the picture at left is a Maya man in gala dress. In the background is a terraced pyramid typical of Pre-Columbian architecture

Principal Maya Cities

At the center of a Maya city were buildings devoted to religious, administrative, and trading activities. All other public buildings were arranged around this core. Farther from the center extended residential neighborhoods, where the ordinary people lived.

At the end of every twenty-year period, or *katún,* the Maya would set up a commemorative stela, a stone monument, with the date of the founding of the city. Thanks to this custom, we know when nearly all of the Maya cities were established.

From Religion to Art

The Maya liked to embellish their cities with deeply harmonious works of great beauty. Of course, their art always had a religious foundation. In the upper-right photo, we see the elegant simplicity of one of the altars of Copán. Below is the Plain of Stelae in Quiriguá. At left is a piece of sculpture from Copán, home of some of the best preserved works of Maya art. The expressiveness of the faces and the purity of the forms show that the sculptors of Copán were superb artists.

Tikal was one of the most elaborate Mayan cities. It lies in the northwest corner of the Petén region, in the rain forests of present-day Guatemala. Today Tikal is protected as one of Guatemala's national parks.

Tikal began as a small town and rose to splendor between the fourth and ninth centuries with the construction of broad plazas, pyramids, and palaces, all covered with hieroglyphics and numerical symbols. Over 300 major structures stood in the heart of the city.

Central Tikal had a population of about 10,000 people. Counting the people in the outlying neighborhoods, the city had thousands more inhabitants.

Tikal was an important commercial center. It traded with Teotihuacan, a city north of the Valley of Mexico. In the ninth century, Tikal began to decline. For a time, groups of people continued to live there, and it was abandoned altogether in the tenth century.

Another important city was Copán. Located on the Copán River in the Petén region of western Honduras, Copán was the Mayas' scientific center. It reached its height around the year A.D. 700 and was abandoned around the tenth century. Spanish explorers discovered the ruins of Copán in the 1700s. It was restored in the mid-1900s.

Copán had sixteen neighborhoods fanning out from its center. In the center is the Acropolis, a collection of pyramids, terraces, temples, and plazas; an esplanade with many stelae and altars; and a stadium for ball games.

From the esplanade rose the great Hieroglyphic Stairway. Its sixty-three steps were covered with hieroglyphic writing. On every tenth step stood a stone statue of an important person or one of the gods.

Quiriguá was a smaller city 30 miles (48 kilometers) to the north. It was an extension, or "vassal city," of Copán. The ruins of Quiriguá were discovered in the 1800s, and excavation began in the early 1900s.

Quiriguá was founded around A.D. 650 and reached its height in the eighth century. It, too, was abandoned in the tenth century. Quiriguá was patterned after most other Maya cities. Residential neighborhoods surrounded a city center that included a great plaza with altars, temples, and stelae dedicated to the gods.

Quiriguá's claim to fame are its spectacular stelae. Stela E is one of the finest stone carvings in the New World. Thirty-five feet (almost 11 meters) tall, it is a masterful carving of lordly figures wearing emblems of rank.

A City of Surprises
The Spaniard Diego García de Palacio discovered the ruins of Copán in 1576. He was utterly astonished. He had been looking for a lost village, and instead he found a great city. Copán's Ceremonial Esplanade is an enormous plaza of about 800 square feet (75 square meters). Three sides are formed by tiers of steps, and the fourth opens to a low hill. Nine stelae and several carved altars stand in the plaza. (*Top*) A portion of the esplanade. (*Bottom*) The wall of one of Copán's temples.

Some Maya settled in the Yucatán peninsula. Their most outstanding sacred city was Chichen Itzá. Like other great Mayan cities, it had a great ceremonial center dotted with pyramids. Other noteworthy structures are the Castle or Temple of Kukulkán, the astronomical observatory, and several ball courts.

The Mayan Ball Game

The ancient Maya played a ball game called *tlachtli*. It was not only a sport, but also a religious ritual. The stakes may have been high. There is evidence to suggest that the losers were sacrificed.

The playing court was rectangular. High on the walls of the longer sides were two vertical stone rings.

Two teams competed in the game, each with seven players. The ball, made of solid rubber, measured 8 to 10 inches (20 to 25 centimeters) in diameter. The object of the game was to pass the ball through one of the stone rings.

As in soccer, the players could use only their shoulders, hips, and knees. If a player used his hands or feet, he was penalized. *Tlachtli* was extremely difficult to play. The winning team was the one that committed the fewest fouls.

The Last Maya
The remains of Tikal, Copán, and Quiriguá reveal how powerful these ancient cities must have been. Even after the Spaniards arrived, the Maya were not completely destroyed. In the Mexican state of Chiapas live the Lacandones, the direct descendants of the Maya. They still speak the Maya language, wear traditional dress, and live by farming. *(Top left)* A view of Tikal. *(Top right)* A stela from Quiriguá. *(Lower right)* A temple in Quiriguá.

Calendar of Festivals
The Maya used two calendars. The *Haab* ordered daily existence. The *Tzolkín* regulated ceremonial life. The picture at left represents the *Tzolkín*.

These Sites Are Part of the World Heritage

Copán: Maya city in Honduras. It reached its height around A.D. 700. Copán was the scientific center of this period. Its ceremonial center, the Acropolis, was a collection of pyramids, terraces, temples, and plazas.

Tikal: Maya city in Guatemala. Tikal was one of the largest and oldest centers of the Maya empire. Its ceremonial center consists of temples, plazas, palaces, and five major pyramids.

Quiriguá: Maya city in Guatemala. Quiriguá is much smaller than the other two cities. Its gigantic stelae and sandstone altars are outstanding.

Glossary

aqueduct: a channel through which water is conveyed

astronomical: having to do with stars, planets, and other objects in the sky

ceramic: made from clay or a similar material and hardened by firing

coming-of-age: the process or ceremony in which a child becomes an adult

deform: to permanently change the shape or outline of something

dowry: a gift given to the groom by the bride's family

drought: a rainless period

esplanade: an open stretch of ground

herbs: plants used as flavorings or as medicines

hieroglyphs: characters, drawings, or symbols used as a writing system

logarithm: in mathematics, the power to which a number is raised to produce another number

loincloth: a short cloth that hangs from a cord around the waist or hips

matchmaker: someone who finds suitable marriage partners for young people who wish to get married

nomadic: traveling from place to place

observatory: a structure from which people can observe the skies or distant land

oracle: a person believed to be speaking for a god in making predictions

plaited: braided

shroud: a long piece of cloth wound around the body

stela: (plural, stelae) a carved stone slab or pillar

terraced: built in a stair-step pattern

umbilical cord: the cord by which a baby is attached to the placenta in its mother's uterus

urn: a vase, such as one used to contain the ashes of a cremated body

Index

Page numbers in boldface type indicate illustrations.

Titles in the World Heritage Series

The Land of the Pharaohs
The Chinese Empire
Ancient Greece
Prehistoric Rock Art
The Roman Empire
Mayan Civilization
Tropical Rain Forests of Central America
Inca Civilization
Prehistoric Stone Monuments
Romanesque Art and Architecture
Great Animal Refuges
Coral Reefs

Photo Credits

Page 3: Juan Antonio Fernandez-Covadonga de Noriega/Incafo; p. 5: J. A. Fernandez-C. de Noriega/Incafo; p. 6: J. A. Fernandez-C. de Noriega/Incafo; p. 7: Loren McIntyre; pp. 8-9: J. A. Fernandez-C. de Noriega/Incafo; p. 11: J. A. Fernandez-C. de Noriega/ Incafo and L. McIntyre; p. 13: J. A. Fernandez-C. de Noriega/Incafo; p. 16: J. A. Fernandez-C. de Noriega/Incafo; p. 19: J. A. Fernandez-C. de Noriega/Incafo and L. McIntyre; pp. 20-21: J. A. Fernandez-C. de Noriega/Incafo; p. 23: J. A. Fernandez-C. de Noriega/ Incafo; p. 25: J. A. Fernandez-C. de Noriega/Incafo; p. 26: J. A. Fernandez-C. de Noriega/ Incafo; p. 27: J. A. Fernandez-C. de Noriega/Incafo; p. 29: J. A. Fernandez-C. de Noriega/Incafo; p. 31: J. A. Fernandez-C. de Noriega/Incafo.

Project Editor, Childrens Press: Ann Heinrichs
Original Text: Pilar Tutor
Subject Consultant: Dr. Robert Pickering
Translator: Deborah Kent
Design: Alberto Caffaratto
Cartography: Modesto Arregui
Drawings: Federico Delicado
Phototypesetting: Publishers Typesetters, Inc.

UNESCO's World Heritage

The United Nations Educational, Scientific, and Cultural Organization (UNESCO) was founded in 1946. Its purpose is to contribute to world peace by promoting cooperation among nations through education, science, and culture. UNESCO believes that such cooperation leads to universal respect for justice, for the rule of law, and for the basic human rights of all people.

UNESCO's many activities include, for example, combatting illiteracy, developing water resources, educating people on the environment, and promoting human rights.

In 1972, UNESCO established its World Heritage Convention. With members from over 100 nations, this international body works to protect cultural and natural wonders throughout the world. These include significant monuments, archaeological sites, geological formations, and natural landscapes. Such treasures, the Convention believes, are part of a World Heritage that belongs to all people. Thus, their preservation is important to us all.

Specialists on the World Heritage Committee have targeted over 300 sites for preservation. Through technical and financial aid, the international community restores, protects, and preserves these sites for future generations.

Volumes in the *World Heritage* series feature spectacular color photographs of various World Heritage sites and explain their historical, cultural, and scientific importance.